Supplement for 1974-6 to Recent Liturgical Revision in the Church of England

by

Colin Buchanan

Vice-Principal of St. John's College, Bramcote, Nottingham

Member of the Church of England Liturgical Commission

GROVE BOOKS

BRAMCOTE NOTTS.

CONTENTS

Page

1. The Church of England (Worship and Doctrine) Measure 1974 .. 4

2. Drafting Bodies 5

3. Events in Synod 8

Appendixes:

1 Chart of Procedures and Progress in Liturgical Revision 16

2 Chronological Table of Liturgical Events in Synod .. 18

3 The New ICET Texts 21

4 Revised Canons B.1 to B.5A 22

5 New Canon B.4A 24

First Impression July 1976

ISSN 0305 3067

ISBN 0 901710 94 6

INTRODUCTION

This booklet stands in close succession to Booklets 14 and 14A, *Recent Liturgical Revision in the Church of England* (April 1973) and *Supplement for 1973-4 to Recent Liturgical Revision in the Church of England* (September 1974). Because it is a supplement, it picks up where the previous supplement left off, and will look odd to those who read it on its own.

Part of it has to be given to the tidying up of the Church of Ehgland (Worship and Doctrine) Measure 1974, the text of which was printed in Booklet 14A. The last stages of authorizing and implementing the Measure and the consequential Canons duly take their place here. But these matters are but the background to the actual process of revision.

From my personal point of view, the two years covered by this supplement are the years the Revision Committees have eaten! This is not in itself a criticism of the system of Revision Committees. It is possible in some cases that hard-headed chairmanship would have got through business in less time and without loss. But the basic problem has been the sheer quantity of days in London needed by the members of the Committees. No doubt the chairman of the Liturgical Commission, Dr. Ronald Jasper, will have noticed the difference when he left Westminster in early Autumn 1975 to become Dean of York! In the period here reviewed there have been Revision Committees on Series 3 Funerals, Morning and Evening Prayer, Collects, and Weddings, and on '1½' Communion also. I doubt if these should have been handled *in toto* on the floor of Synod, so I can only wring my hands over the cost (which must be thousands of pounds in total) and the amount of time of the Committees. It is a function of geography—in Provinces and countries two or three thousand miles across no-one would expect to appear before Revision Committees of General Synod at the drop of a hat! Indeed in most such countries General Synod itself only meets every other year. In England the Synod meets three times a year, and Committees function non-stop in between. Whilst I would hate to be out of it, I continue to wonder whether the process could not be handled more efficiently and cheaply.

The two years have also found me giving space elsewhere to many of the items charted in this booklet. In January 1975. I started to edit and publish the monthly *News of Liturgy* which is circularized to the great majority of those who take the booklets on standing order. I have also edited and published *Further Anglican Liturgies 1968-75* (Grove Books, May 1975) and this too contains much that is relevant to this booklet. Neither of these publications seemed to me to justify omitting germane material here.

Having got that off my chest, I add that the presentation of this booklet is similar to that of its predecessors. As I said at the end of the introduction to booklet 14A: 'The same principles have determined what is in and what is out; the same insistence is necessary that I write not as a chronicler but as a journalist—though, I hope, an accurate one; and the same debt of thanks must be expressed to the many who have helped me in the provison of information.'

Colin Buchanan, 22 July 1976

1. THE CHURCH OF ENGLAND (WORSHIP AND DOCTRINE) MEASURE 1974

In September 1974, when Booklet 14A was completed, the Worship and Doctrine Measure had passed the General Synod and the Ecclesiastical Committee of Parliament, and was awaiting a General Election in order that there should *be* a Parliament to give it the force of law.[1] The election duly occurred on 10 October 1974, and the Measure started forward again on its progress. It was debated in the House of Lords on 14 November 1974, where it was introduced by Dr. Michael Ramsey on his last day in office as Archbishop of Canterbury. After a four hour debate the Measure was agreed without a division, and then went to the Commons.[2] The Commons debated it on 4 December 1974, giving seven hours to the debate.

In the Commons it became clear that there was a residue of opposition which could not be easily conciliated. Some opposed the Measure because (like Mr. Enoch Powell) they thought the State ought to own and control the Church. Others seemed to think they were debating the merits and demerits of Series 3 Communion.[3] Even those in favour of the Measure did not always inspire confidence that they had understood it. But it finally gained approval by 145 votes to 45, and received the Royal Assent on 12 December 1974.

Under Clause 7(2) of the Measure[4] it was to come into force on a day to be named by the Archbishops of Canterbury and York. They gave little advance notice of when it would be, but early in August 1975 it was announced it would come into force on 1 September 1975.

1 September 1975 thus marked the final repeal of all the Acts and Measures from the sixteenth century and onwards which were listed in the Schedules to the Measure,[5] most notably the Act of Uniformity 1662 and the Church of England (Alternative and Other Services) Measure 1965. It brought into force the amending Canons on Worship, and on Assent or Subscription.[6] And it left the text of the 1662 Prayer Book (but not the rubrics) in the custody of Parliament, never to be repealed until Parliament itself should so direct.[7]

1 It will be recalled that a 'Measure' is a Parliamentary enactment on ecclesiastical matters, which is drafted and approved in General Synod before being submitted for a single reading in each of the two Houses of Parliament. See also Booklet 14, p.4. The text of this Measure is printed as an apprendix to Booklet 14A, pp.18-21.

2 The system does not provide for emendation by either House, but only for a single reading in each, which thus constitutes a right of veto, but no more.

3 One even commented 'I am sorry that, despite criticism to the contrary, no Church authority thought fit to place a copy of Series 3 in the Library of the House. Unfortunately, as I do not have a copy, I have been unable to study it.' (*Hansard* Vol. 882, No. 31. Col. 1638). The errors here are legion—notably, that it was not Series 3 which was being debated and that in Westminster at least four shops within 300 yards of the Commons would have sold the Hon. Member a copy for 8p!

4 See Booklet 14A, p.21.

5 See Booklet 14A pp.21-2.

6 For the main outcome of the Canon on Worship see pp.22-4 below. For the Declaration of Assent see Booklet 14A, p.24.

7 For a description of the way in which this feature was entrenched, see Booklet 14A pp.5-6.

2. DRAFTING BODIES

(a) The Liturgical Commission[1]

In September 1974, the Liturgical Commission had just cleared the draft of Series 3 Morning and Evening Prayer through the House of Bishops, and it was to be published (as GS 215) on 10 October 1974. The subsequent work of the Commission has been as follows:

A. Series 1 and 2 Revised Holy Communion[2] was published on 2 January 1975.[3] This was debated in General Synod in July 1975, February 1976 and July 1976, and is now authorized from 1 November 1976.[4]

B. The modern language collects were completed in December 1974, passed by the House of Bishops in January 1975, and published[5] on 10 April 1975. They were debated in Synod in July 1975 and July 1976, and are due to receive Final Approval in November 1976.

C. Contrary to all expectations[6], the Liturgical Commission was asked by the Archbishops to complete Series 3 Infant Baptism. This was done in March 1975, and the report was published[7] on 29 May 1975. It was on the agenda for General Synod in both July 1975 and November 1975, but in January 1976 the Standing Committee spotted (what had been abundantly clear all along[8]) that any debates on this text would be confused with those on the Initiation questions,[9] so the service was removed from the agenda.[10]

1 The work listed here should be read in continuity with that listed in Booklet 14A, p.4.

2 *Alternative Services Series 1 and 2 Revised Holy Communion: A Report by the Liturgical Commission of the General Synod of the Church of England* (GS 217) (S.P.C.K., 35p).

3 The text in its draft form is reprinted in *Further Anglican Liturgies 1968-1975* (Grove Books, 1975) pp.61-9, where it is preceded by a brief historical introduction. See also Booklet 14A, pp.8-9, referring to Booklet 14, p.18.

4 The two-colour authorized booklets should be available from 21 October 1976, when they are to be published by the S.P.C.K. and priviliged presses at 25p.

5 *Collects to accompany the Lectionary for Holy Communion Series 3: A Report by the Liturgical Commission of the General Synod of the Church of England* (GS 230) (S.P.C.K., 50p). This is now reprinted at 70p.

6 See Booklet 14A, p.4.

7 *Alternative Services Series 3 Infant Baptism: A Report by the Liturgical Commission of the General Synod of the Church of England* (GS 225) (S.P.C.K., 20p).

8 The Commission says this discreetly in its Introduction, where in the first paragraph it anticipates the confusion if the Initiation factors catch up with the debate on the service. I personally was less discreet in Booklet 37—*The Liturgy for Infant Baptism (Series 3)*—where I spelled out the problems on p.10. I spelled them out again retrospectively in a speech in the debate on the Standing Committee's Report on the Business on the Agenda on 24 February 1976, but got little change.

9 See pp.14-15 below.

10 It is doubtful whether it can come back on until 1977, and by then it might just as well have waited for the adult services.

D. The Wedding service was completed in December 1974, and after going to the House of Bishops, it was published[1] on 29 May 1975. It was debated in General Synod in November 1975, and at the time of writing is still before its Revision Committee, to be brought to Synod for Provisional Approval in November 1976.

E. The Calendar and Lectionary provisions were completed in December 1975, approved by the House of Bishops in January 1976, and published[2] on 3 June 1976. They were on the agenda for the July 1976 Group of Sessions of General Synod, but were not reached.

F. A draft Ordinal was completed in December 1975, and sent to the House of Bishops. It is still under consideration in that House.[3]

G. Members of the Liturgical Commission contributed to *The Eucharist To-Day: Essays on Series 3* edited R. C. D. Jasper, published by S.P.C.K. in November 1974.

In December 1975 the last meeting of the Liturgical Commission with its then membership was held. The appointment of each member lapsed in the New Year of 1976, and the new Standing Committee (of the General Synod which was elected in October 1975) took responsibility for agreeing names with the two Archbishops. No meeting of the Commission was held in March 1976, and from 1976 onwards the Commission will only meet residentially three times a year.

The following were appointed to serve on the Liturgical Commission till 28 February 1981 (those marked with an asterisk being members of the previous Commission): *The Dean of York (The Very Rev. R. C. D. Jasper) (Chairman), *the Rev. C. O. Buchanan, *Mr. H. R. M. Craig, *Canon G. J. Cuming, *Dr. D. L. Frost, the Bishop of Gloucester (the Rt. Rev. John Yates), *the Rev. D. C. Gray, the Rev. Dr. D. M. Hope, the Bishop of Jarrow (the Rt. Rev. A. K. Hamilton), the Rev. Prof. J. Kinsley, *Mrs. J. M. Mayland, Dss. D. McClatchey, the Rev. R. D. Silk, *Canon E. C. Whitaker, the Rev. J. D. Wilkinson. Those not re-appointed (in most, but not all,

[1] *Alternative Services Series 3 The Wedding Service: A Report by the Liturgical Commission of the General Synod of the Church of England* (GS 228) (S.P.C.K. 25p).

[2] *The Calendar, Lectionary and Rules to Order the Service 1976: A Report by the Liturgical Commission of the General Synod of the Church of England* (GS 292) (S.P.C.K. £1·95).

[3] Bishops obviously have a very particular concern about ordination services, and they are expressing it in their close and continuing scrutiny of the Commission's draft. There also remains ahead a sunken rock which seems to have escaped notice so far. A new Ordinal could be an 'alternative' service, but it could never be *the* Church of England's Ordinal without the rescinding of the 1662 Ordinal (which would require a Measure going through Parliament—see p.4 above). It is not clear yet whether alternative Ordinals sufficiently fulfil the foundational doctrinal role which it is assumed (as, e.g., in the 'Ten Propositions' on Unity) an Ordinal should have.

cases, at their own request) are[1] the Bishop of Derby (the Rt. Rev. C. W. J. Bowles), the Rev. J. L. Houlden, the Bishop of Woolwich (the Rt. Rev. Michael Marshall), Mrs. E. M. Montefiore, the Dean of St. Albans (the Very Rev. P. C. Moore), the Rev. L. E. H. Stephens-Hodge, Canon C. V. Taylor. Mrs. Barbara Ebdale replaced Miss Daphne Fraser as secretary in Autumn 1974.

The new Commission met for the first time in June 1976, and is engaged on devising questionnaires on Series 3 Holy Communion, writing alternative eucharistic prayers, compiling liturgical provision for the ministry to the sick, and taking responsibility for bringing together the contents of the 'Alternative Service Book'.

(b) The Joint Liturgical Group (JLG)[2]
The JLG published on 10 July 1975 *Worship and the Child*[3], and has almost completed the 'ecumenical eucharistic prayer' mentioned in Booklet 14A. This is to be published as part of a larger collection of occasional prayers, litanies and intercessions.

(c) The International Consultation on English Texts (ICET)[4]
ICET completed in 1974 a conservative revision of the ICET texts which were in *Prayers We Have in Common* (1970 and 1971). A year elapsed between completion and publication, but the texts and translations were finally published on 10 July 1975.[5] The new texts have been adopted in overseas Anglican uses[6], and in the new Methodist ones in England.[7] But they have not so far been considered for inclusion in the Church of England's services.

(d) Synodical Working-Parties
General Synod has in the period under review had working-parties considering an 'Alternative Service Book' and the Diocesan returns from the Initiation debate. Each of these is reported under the relevant heading below.

(e) Frost and Macintosh
The work on a 'Modern Liturgical Psalter' progresses. The first samples of this modern Psalter were published in *Twenty-Five Psalms from a Modern Liturgical Psalter.*[8] Further samples were included in Series 3 Funerals and Series 3 Morning and Evening Prayer. The whole project has been accepted for the 1980 'Alternative Service Book', and it should be published in its entirety in 1977.

1 Leslie Houlden and Cyril Taylor are retained as 'consultants'. There is also a variety of observers from other Anglican Churches, and from the Church of Rome.
2 See Booklet 14, pp.11-12, and Booklet 14A p.15.
3 Edited R. C. D. Jasper (S.P.C.K. 95p).
4 See Booklet 14, pp.12-13, and Booklet 14A, p.15.
5 *Prayers We Have in Common* (S.P.C.K. 65p).
6 As, e.g. in the 1974 Canadian *Alternative Liturgy*, the South African *Liturgy 1975*, and PECUSA draft 1976 Book of Common Prayer.
7 See *The Methodist Service Book* (Methodist Publishing House 1975) pp.B.10 etc. The alterations to the texts in the 1974 version are tabulated in the appendix on p.21 below.
8 Published by the Church Information Office in 1973 at 55p.

3. EVENTS IN SYNOD

Synod has had a large amount of liturgical business to do in the period under review and has fully needed (but usually not obtained) the 'one full day' in each group of sessions which was recommended in the report on *The Future Course of Liturgical Revision.*[1] The procedure has been handled in accordance with the Standing Orders approved on 21 February 1973[2]—and the Standing Orders have come into their own with a proliferation of Revision Committees.[3] The period has also been marked by the dissolution of the first General Synod in July 1975, and the election of the second, which first met in November 1975, to serve until July 1980. The new Synod elected a new Standing Committee, and the new Standing Committee advised the Archbishops on the appointment of a new Liturgical Commission[4] to serve till 28 February 1981.

In the listing below the chronological sequence has been ignored, and a chronological table of events along with exact voting details is to be found in appendix 2 on page 18.[5]

Constitutional Matters

The Synod gave Final Approval in February 1975 to the two Amending Canons requisite to bring into operation the provisions of the Worship and Doctrine Measure.[6] They were promulged and executed at the July 1975 Group of Sessions and they came into force on the day the Measure itself came into force, 1 September 1975. There also proved to be a need for a Canon providing for the approval of Collects, Lectionaries etc. apart from their being attached to specific services. A new Canon to provide for this (B.4A) was Generally Approved, then given formal Provisional Approval in the same week in July 1975, it was then given Final Approval in November 1975, and was promulged and executed in February 1976. Its text is to be found in appendix 5 on page 24 below. The whole set of new Canons is now available in a loose-leaf binder.[7]

Series 1 and 2

The original Series 1 services had all either lapsed or been renewed by November 1973.[8] Series 2 services were extended in recent sessions of Synod as follows (in each case until 31 December 1979):

Series 2 (Revised) Morning and Evening Prayer: Provisional Approval, February 1975; Final Approval, July 1975.[9]

Series 2 Holy Communion: Provisional Approval, February 1976; Final Approval, July 1976.[10]

[1] (GS 161). See Booklet 14A, p.8.

[2] See Booklet 14A, p.13, and pp.16-17 below for a diagrammatic presentation.

[3] See the Standing Orders in Booklet 14A, p.13, and also p.3 above.

[4] For the details see pp.6-7 above.

[5] This reverses the presentation in Booklet 14A, but seemed preferable.

[6] The full text of the amended Canons on Worship is set out in appendix 4 on pp.22-4 below. The text of the Declaration of Assent is in Booklet 14A, p.24.

[7] *The Canons of the Church of England* (C.I.O., 1976, £3·24, inc. V.A.T.). The first supplement to these (including the new B.4A) was published on 1 July 1976 (Church House Bookshop, 22p. inc. V.A.T.).

[8] See Booklet 14A, p.16.

[9] For exact dates and voting figures see p.19 below.

[10] For exact dates and voting figures see p.20 below.

However, the main service in this category was 'Series 1 and 2 Revised Holy Communion'. This service was first suggested by Dr. Jasper in the first debate on Series 3 Holy Communion in November 1971[1], and the actual task of constructing it came to the Liturgical Commission after the debate in July 1973 on 'The Future Course of Liturgical Revision'.[2] The resolution passed then was:

> 'That the General Synod would welcome an opportunity to consider the desirability of replacing Series 1 and Series 2 Holy Communion with a single rite.'

The Commission therefore drafted a composite service, which passed the House of Bishops in Summer 1974, and was published on 2 January 1975.[3] It was briefly debated at 'General Consideration' on 1 July 1975 and was remitted to a Revision Committee. The Revision Committee sat for some months and reported to the February 1976 Group of Sessions, with a report (GS 217Y) explaining the changes proposed and the revised text itself (GS 217X). The Revision Stage was taken on 26 February 1976, and a few amendments were made in full Synod. The Synod then gave Provisional Approval. The House of Bishops made further changes[4] before Synod received it, and gave it Final Approval on 14 July 1976.[5] The service is due at the time of writing to be published on 21 October 1976[6] and is authorized from 1 November 1976 to 31 December 1979.

This service was originally intended to 'replace' Series 1 and Series 2 as separate services. This in turn meant that the proposal to renew the life of Series 2 as a separate service in February and July 1976 was probably, strictly speaking, otiose.[7] However, the actual choice between the rites has now been postponed until 1979. It will be noted that the proposed 'Alternative Service Book' is due to contain the composite rite ('1½', as it is frequently called) rather than Series 2.

1 See Booklets 14, p.18, and 14A pp.4, 9, 16.

2 See Booklet 14A, p.9.

3 The full title was *Alternative Services Series 1 and 2 Revised Holy Communion: A Report by the Liturgical Commission of the General Synod of the Church of England* (GS 217) (S.P.C.K.). The original text is also printed in C. O. Buchanan *Further Anglican Liturgies 1968-1975* (Grove Books, 1975) pp.61-9, where it is preceded by an introduction.

4 The House of Bishops has the right to make slight drafting amendments and it changed one word at this stage in Series 3 Communion (see Booklet 14, p.28). But on this occasion the Bishops made no less than *six* amendments, at least one of which (the restoration as an option of the traditional ending of the Prayer of Humble Access—by a vote of 19 to 18 in that House! (See GS 217Z, the report of the House of Bishops)) irritated the Synod considerably.

5 The full voting figures are on p.20 below. It will be noted that '1½' only obtained its two-thirds majority in the House of Clergy by the narrowest possible margin. I personally, who had little heart for the service and very nearly opposed it, in fact abstained (being one of the members in charge).

6 It will be published by the S.P.C.K. and the Privileged Presses at 25p.

7 Indeed it might be argued not only that '1½' was intended to *replace* Series 2 (see Booklet 14A, p.9), but also that no-one who favoured the Series 2 'route' through '1½' would be tempted to obtain the new booklets, containing all the options of a Series 1 type, whilst the simple Series 2 ran on. But it was pleaded that it was tidier to take all services to 1979. The voting on Final Approval is on p.20 below.

Series 3

The first Series 3 service was Holy Communion, authorized for four years from 1 February 1973. On 14 July 1976 Provisional Approval was given to the extension of its period until 31 December 1979. Final Approval will be sought in November 1976. The Liturgical Commission is devising a questionnaire upon this service, with a view to minor revisions of it before its inclusion in the projected 'Alternative Service Book'.

The second Series 3 service was the Funeral service (technically Funeral service*s* in the plural). They were before a Revision Committee in Summer 1974[1], and the report of the Revision Committee (GS 147Y) along with the revised text itself (GS 147A) came before the Synod on 7 November 1974. A few small further amendments were made in full Synod at the Revision Stage, then Provisional Approval was given. Final Approval followed on 5 February 1975[2], and the services were authorized for four years from 1 June 1975. The mauve glossy-covered two-coloured booklets[3] were published on 18 May 1975. On 14 July 1976 Provisional Approval was given for the extension to 31 December 1979, and final Approval will come in November 1976.

The third Series 3 service was Morning and Evening Prayer. This was published as a report on 10 October 1974[4], given 'General Consideration' on 7 November 1974, and remitted to a Revision Committee. This Committee worked very fast, and was able to report to the February 1975 Group of Sessions of Synod. Its Report (GS 215Y), which includes a summary of the changes in the text, was debated on 5 February 1975, a few small amendments were made in full Synod, and then Provisional Approval was given. Final Approval followed on 1 July 1975[5], the yellow glossy-covered booklets were published on 18 October 1975[6], and the services were authorized for a period from 1 November 1975 to 31 December 1979.

The next Series 3 services to come from the Liturgical Commission were the Wedding Service[7] and Infant Baptism service[8] published on 29 May 1975. Both were on the agenda for the July Group of Sessions in 1975, but neither was reached. The Wedding service was given 'General Consideration' on 13 November 1975, and remitted to a Revision Committee. This Committee has at the time of writing met six times and has still

1 See Booklet 14A, p.14, note 2.
2 Full figures are on p.18 below.
3 AS 360 and AS 362, published by S.P.C.K. at 16p and 35p respectively—the second-named being in a larger format.
4 *Alternative Services Series 3 Morning and Evening Prayer: A Report by the Liturgical Commission of the General Synod of the Church of England* (GS 215) (S.P.C.K. 75p). Although this was published in October 1974, it *was* handled immediately by Synod, contrary to the expectations set out in Booklet 14A, p.17.
5 Full figures are on p.19 below.
6 It was published by the S.P.C.K. and the Privileged Presses (AS 310) at 25p.
7 *Alternative Services Series 3 Wedding Service: A Report by the Liturgical Commission of the Church of England* (GS 228) (S.P.C.K. 25p).
8 *Alternative Services Series 3 Infant Baptism: A Report by the Liturgical Commission of the General Synod of the Church of England* (GS225) (S.P.C.K. 20p).

not completed its work. It should report to the November 1976 Group of Sessions, and after the Revision Stage the service should receive Provisional Approval. Final Approval could then follow in February 1977, with authorization from, say, 1 June 1977, and printed copies of the text two weeks earlier. The Infant Baptism Service was not reached in November 1975 and was finally taken *off* the agenda of Synod in February 1976.[1]

Collects and **Calendar, Lectionary and Rules to Order the Service**

The report on the collects was published on 10 April 1975[2]. The collects were based on the themes for the Sundays, and related closely to those in the 1969 report *The Calendar and Lessons*[3], which itself drew them from *The Daily Office* of the Joint Liturgical Group. The South African Liturgical Committee published *Modern Collects* in 1972, and these and other modernizations were laid under contribution. The Commission's proposals received 'General Consideration' (amounting to about nine minutes in all) in the closing stages of the last session of the Synod of 1970-1975, on 4 July 1975. Its Revision Committee reported[4] in time for the February 1976 Group of Sessions, but the report was not reached on the agenda. The Revision Stage was thus taken on 14 July 1976, and in full Synod several minor amendments were made to the Committee's text, a few of them bringing the material back into the form originally proposed by the Liturgical Commission. Provisional Approval was then given (*nem. con.* as far as could be discerned), and the collects are remitted to the House of Bishops to bring them before Synod in November 1976 for Final Approval. They will be authorized under the terms of the new Canon B.4A,[5] which permits such material to be authorized without being attached to any particular service. If they are to be published as a separate booklet they could be authorized from, say, 1 February 1977, and printed copies could be available two weeks earlier. But they could be held back to be added to the calendar and lectionary material.

The last report of the Liturgical Commission to come into the public eye is that on the calendar and lectionary, published on 3 June 1976.[6] This was on the agenda for the July 1976 Group of Sessions of General Synod but was not reached on that occasion. It is a comprehensive provision, fulfilling the terms of the motions passed in the debate on 20 February 1974.[7] This can be shown by inspection. The only appropriate material missing from the comprehensive provision is the collects, referred to in the paragraph above.

1 See p.4 above.

2 *Collects to accompany the Lectionary for Holy Communion Series 3: A Report by the Liturgical Commission of the General Synod of the Church of England.* (GS 230) (S.P.C.K. 50p, now in second impression 70p).

3 The 'Orange Book'. See Booklet 14, pp.30-1.

4 *General Synod Collects Series 3: Report of the Revision Committee* (GS 230Y) (Church House Bookshop 37p).

5 See pp.6 and 8 above and 24 below.

6 *The Calendar, Lectionary and Rules to Order the Service: A Report by the Liturgical Commission of the General Synod of the Church of England* (GS 292) (S.P.C.K. £1·95).

7 See Booklet 14A, p.10.

The 'Alternative Service Book'

In the debate on 'The Future Course of Liturgical Revision' on 3 July 1973[1], the Synod passed the following motion:

> 'That the House of Bishops and the Standing Committee be asked to set up a working party to draw up detailed plans for the issue of a People's Service Book, and to report its proposals in due course to the General Synod'.

A working party was set up under the chairmanship of the Bishop of Durham, and it first met in May 1974. They drew up a questionnaire and upon advice sent certain proposals, with the questions attached, to 620 parishes. The book was to be an 'alternative service book', containing no 1662 material, with a comprehensive range of services, and to be in use roughly for the decade 1980-90. Of the 408 replies, 276 replied that it should be published and 115 that it should not. 222 considered they would be likely to obtain copies for congregational use and 165 that they would not.[2] On the basis of this the working party decided they had enough support to proceed.[3]

They then produced recommendations that the new book should be available in two versions, though both would be fairly full versions. The contents as proposed read as follows:

Both versions

Morning and Evening Prayer
Liturgical Psalter
References to the Lections for Morning and Evening Prayer
Holy Communion Series 1 and 2 Revised
Holy Communion Series 3
Collects
Baptism and Confirmation
Wedding Service
Funeral Services

Shorter versions only

References to Lections for Holy Communion

Longer version only

Lections for Holy Communion
Catechism
Ordinal

1 See Booklet 14A, pp.8-9.

2 The numbers do not total 408 presumably because not all parishes gave distinct answers to the questions.

3 There was criticism in the debate which followed, on the grounds that the positive responses, as a proportion of the 620 parishes which were polled, were inadequate as a basis for proceeding. There was also criticism to the effect that it was relatively easy for parishes to say they *would be likely* to purchase fairly expensive books (the Working Party indicated over 1,000 pages for the longer version, and at least 600 for the shorter), whereas *actually* purchasing in 1980 might not be half as easy.

The working party did consider the possibility of a lightweight 'interim book' and so included questions about this in the questionnaire. But the responses were unenthusiastic, and they did not recommend this to Synod. The report was published in January 1976.[1] It was debated in Synod on 27 February 1976, when the main motion was:

> 'That the Synod accepts the proposal for an Alternative Service Book set out in paragraph 42 of the Report of the Working Party.'

Various attempts were made to amend this—one being to include parts of 1662, and another to delay decision until 1978.[2] A third waited in the wings, to be moved if the Bishop of Durham's motion failed, and this would have continued the role of booklets and encouraged any publisher to provide his own compilations of official material.[3] In the debate the Bishop of Durham held all these would-be amenders (or wreckers) at bay, and his motion was passed by a heavy majority. The Synod then passed a consequential motion:

> 'That the Standing Committee be instructed to take such steps as it thinks fit to secure publication of the Book, and to report to Synod.'

Responsibility for the continuance of the task therefore lies with Standing Committee. The actual compilation of the book will no doubt be the task of the Liturgical Commission.

Christian Initiation

In July 1974 the Synod referred certain questions to the dioceses[4], and they had to respond by 1 January 1976. The returns were too complex for Synod to handle them in February 1976, but the results were tabulated in *Christian Initiation: Results of the Reference to the Diocesan Synods: 1974-75* (GS 291A)[5] in early March 1976. This included the Diocesan

1 *An Alternative Service Book: The Report of the Working Party appointed by the Standing Committee of the General Synod* (GS 284) (Church House Bookshop, 37p).

2 This delaying amendment was my own. Its purpose was to enable all the material to be included in the book to be scrutinized in its own right, before it should be included in the book. Thus the calendar material (which would undoubtedly be needed) was hardly mentioned by the Working Party, and was not included in its proposals; the 'Modern Liturgical Psalter' (see p.4 above) has certainly not yet been tried by the Church; and Adult Baptism and Confirmation, and the Ordinal, have not been published in any form at all. Additionally, one of my chief hesitations about the actual contents proposed, '1½' Holy Communion, has only just scraped its two-thirds majority in the House of Clergy on Final Approval, and must obviously count as a doubtful starter for the proposed book.

3 A point made by two or three speakers in the debate was that, in the original debate on 'The Future Course of Liturgical Revision' in July 1974, Synod had also passed a motion 'That the General Synod instructs the Standing Committee to provide at a later date an opportunity for the Synod to give further consideration to the proposal that instead of authorizing a new (or alternative) Prayer Book, it should simply content itself with authorizing particular forms of service.' If this proposal had ever been incorporated into the debate as a platform motion, it would have provided the basis for the alternative policy mentioned above.

4 The full details of these are in Booklet 14A, pp.10-13.

5 Published by the Church House Bookshop at 32p.

voting on the resolutions on which the dioceses were asked to vote, and also the full text of resolutions about initiation (particularly about infant baptism) which had been devised and passed additionally in 23 Synods. In brief the voting on the official resolutions showed a strong desire for a service of Thanksgiving for the Birth of a Child, no desire for a service of Blessing of a Child, divided voting on whether to admit children to communion before the age of 'a mature Profession of Faith', and equally divded opinion on whether in such a case to admit them to communion on the basis of baptism alone. There was little support for the alternative proposal that they should have anointing or the laying on of hands with their infant baptism as a basis for admission to communion.

The Standing Committee asked a small subcommittee to look at the returns in order to know what to propose to Synod. The Standing Committee then adopted the report and published it in June 1976 as *Christian Initiation: Follow-up of the Reference to the Diocesan Synods 1974-75* (GS 291).[1] This report said there seemed little desire for a change in baptismal policies[2], but that Synod should be recommended to ask for a Service of Thanksgiving for the Birth of a Child. A change in Initiation patterns would only be warranted on a 'permissive' basis—i.e. with two different disciplines living alongside each other, and dioceses and parishes only adopting a new pattern of initiation when they themselves wanted to.

In the debate on 14 July 1976 the first motion was passed on a show of hands virtually *nem. con.:*

> 'That this Synod considers it desirable that a form of Service of Thanksgiving for the Birth of a Child should be provided for general use throughout the Church of England both where the child is subsequently to be baptized and also where the child is not to be baptized, provided that in such a service both the desirability of, and the distinction from, Holy Baptism are made clear, and requests the House of Bishops to ask the Liturgical Commission to prepare a draft for consideration by the Synod at an early date.'

The second motion was the crucial one. It ran as follows:

> 'That this Synod, accepting that full sacramental participation within the Church may precede a mature Profession of Faith, supports the proposition that alternative provision should be made for the ordering of initiation practice within the Church of England, provided that any revised order is set within a continuing framework of training for the Christian life.'

This motion was ultimately defeated [3] as follows:

	Ayes	*Noes*
House of Bishops	17	27
House of Clergy	83	132
House of Laity	86	112

[1] Published by the Church House Bookshop at 20p.

[2] 16 Dioceses had passed resolutions on infant baptism, of which only one (Southwell) had seemed at all directly critical of the General Synod resolution of 22 February 1974.

[3] The reasons for this were probably threefold:

1. Many were opposed in their own persons to the principle.
2. Some who favoured the principle recognized they could only get it if they were prepared to accept the former of the two alternative patterns of initiation then being attached to it (which they were not).
3. Some favoured the principle in their own persons, but thought it improper to proceed on a 'permissive' basis, with only half-hearted support in the dioceses.

As a result the consequential motions, about alternative patterns and the implementation of them, all lapsed. The Bishop of Newcastle then moved a 'fall-back' motion of his own:

> 'The Diocesan Bishops, in consultation with their Synods, be invited to make wider use of their discretion already allowed under Canon B.27 so as to admit younger children to confirmation when so requested; and to take steps to encourage the periodic renewal of Baptismal Vows in adult life, especially by those who have been baptized and confirmed in childhood.'

This did not go unchallenged. The Bishop of Derby and others pointed out that any discretion[1] existed even without the motion, and as 'discretion' it should not be too formalized by motions. There was some fear that the upshot would be the lowering of the age of a 'mature Profession of Faith', but on a show of hands the motion was passed. Thus the Church of England closed the door upon a concept of child-communion, which at one time had seemed to have a tide running heavily in its favour.[2] Some other motions moved by individual members of Synod were not reached, and may come in November 1976.[3]

[1] The 'discretion' in Canon B.27 merely means that no minimum age is stated, and that ministers shall not present any but those who have come to 'years of discretion', but the same restriction is not apparently laid upon bishops . . .

[2] The *individual* count in the diocesan returns in GS 191A suggested quite a heavy majority in favour.

[3] The three motions already tabled which are yet to come are:

1. (By the Rev. C. O. Buchanan, on behalf of Southwell Diocesan Synod):
   'That this Synod, endorsing the forms of interrogation in Series 2 and draft Series 3 Infant Baptism Services, desires that there should be a re-examination of the conditions upon which infants are accepted for baptism.'
2. (By Mr. J. R. Bradshaw of Salisbury diocese):
   'That the General Synod adheres to the view that Infant Baptism should continue to be available to the children of all parents who are willing to make the requisite promises: and rejects the words "and able" which were inserted after the word "willing" in its predecessor's resolution of February 1974.'
3. (By the Rev. P. S. Dawes of Chelmsford diocese):
   'That the Standing Committee be invited to introduce a draft Canon for amendment of Canon B.21 to provide that instead of the words "[every minister] shall from time to time administer the sacrament of Holy Baptism upon Sundays or other Holy Days or immediately after public worship" there be substituted words to the effect that "[every minister] shall *normally* administer the sacrament of Holy Baptism upon Sundays at public worship' ".

APPENDIX 1

CHART OF PROCEDURES IN LITURGICAL REVISION

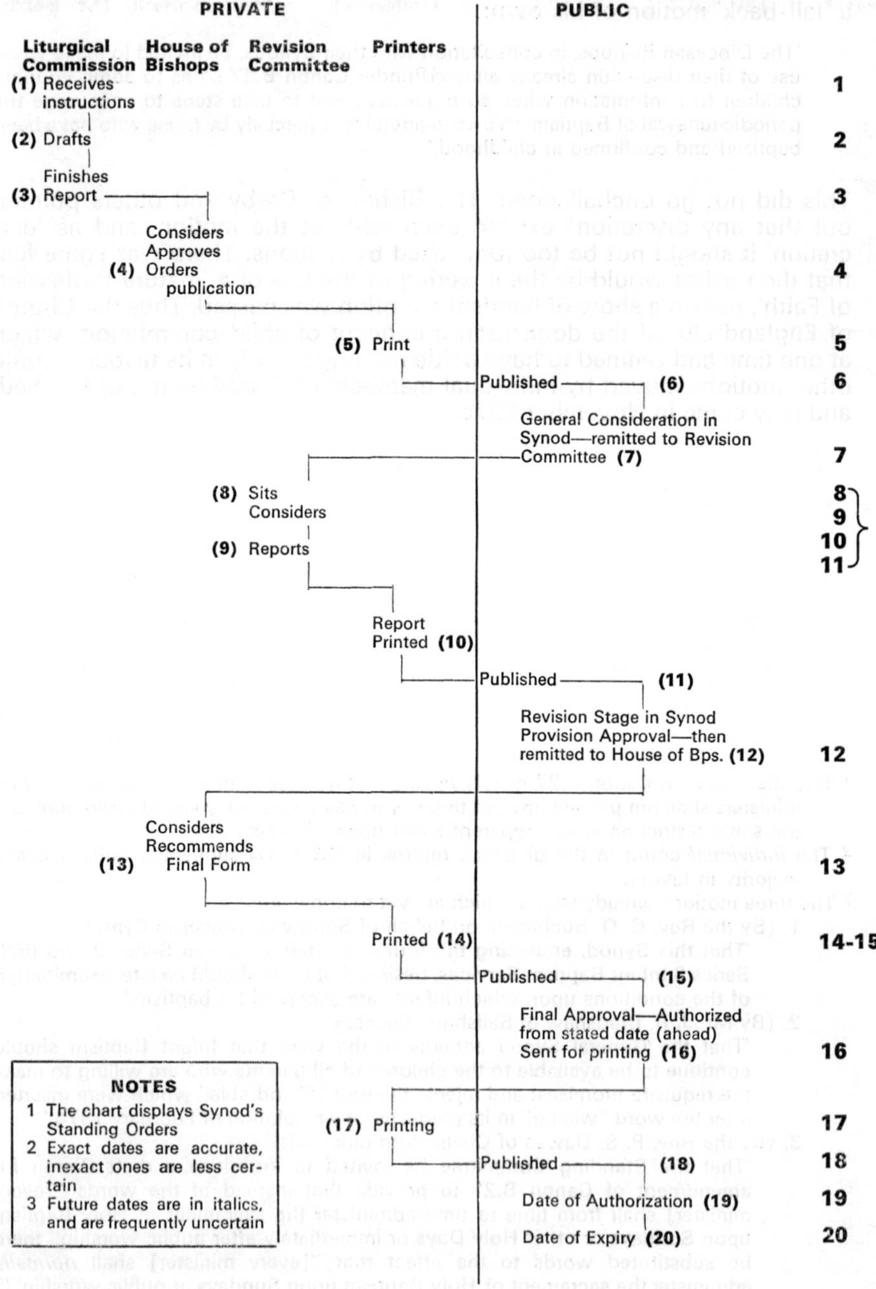

PROCEDURES AND PROGRESS IN LITURGICAL REVISION

PROGRESS WITH ACTUAL SERVICES

ieral 3	MP/EP 3	HC '1½'	Collects 3	Matrimony 3	Inf Baptism 3
9	1972	1973	1972	972	1971
1-2	1973-4	1972-4	1972-4	11972-4	1971-5
1972	Jun 1974	Jun 1974	Dec 1974	Dec 1974	Dec 1974
1973	Sep 1974	Summer 1974	Jan 1975	Jan 1975	Jan 1975
/Mar 1973	Sep 1974	Oct/Dec 1974	Feb/Mar 1975	Feb/Apr 1975	Feb/Apr 1975
Apr 1973	10 Oct 1974	2 Jan 1975	10 Apr 1975	29 May 1975	29 May 1975
Feb 1972	7 Nov 1974	1 Jul 1975	4 Jul 1975	13 Nov 1975	?
nmer 1974	Nov/Dec 1974	Oct 1975- Jan 1976	Oct 1975- Jan 1976	*Feb/Sep 1976*	?
lov 1974	7 Feb 1975	26 Feb 1976	14 Jul 1976	*Nov 1976*	?
1975	May 1975	May 1976	*Autumn 1976*	*Jan 1977*	?
eb 1975	1 Jul 1975	14 Jul 1976	*Mar 1976*	*Feb 1977*	?
r/Apr 1975	Aug/Sep 1975	*Aug/Sep 1976*	*Dec 1976*	*Mar/Apr 1977*	
May 1975	18 Oct 1975	*21 Oct 1976*	*Jan 1977*	*May 1977*	
un 1975	1 Nov 1975	*1 Nov 1976*			
May 1979	*31 Dec 1979*	*31 Dec 1979*		*31 Dec 1979*	

APPENDIX 2 CHRONOLOGICAL TABLE OF LITURGICAL EVENTS IN SYNOD, NOVEMBER 1974 TO JULY 1976

At the **November 1974** Group of Sessions the following action was taken:

On Thursday 7 November 1974:

General Consideration:

Series 3 Morning and Evening Prayer[1]

Provisional Approval:

Series 3 Funerals[2]

At the **February 1975** Group of Sessions the following action was taken:

On Tuesday 4 February 1975:

Final Approval:

Draft Amending Canon (No. 3) (Worship)[3]

The voting on this Canon was:

	Ayes	*Noes*
House of Bishops	24	0
House of Clergy	136	4
House of Laity	106	2

Draft Amending Canon (No. 4) (Assent or Subscription to Doctrine)[4]

The voting on this Canon was:

	Ayes	*Noes*
House of Bishops	23	0
House of Clergy	115	1
House of Laity	89	2

On Wednesday 5 February 1975:

Final Approval:

Series 3 Funeral Services (for four years from 1 June 1975):

The voting on these services was:

	Ayes	*Noes*
House of Bishops	20	0
House of Clergy	107	11
House of Laity	73	7

Provisional Approval:

Series 3 Morning and Evening Prayer

Series 2 (Revised) Morning and Evening Prayer (extension)

[1] These were in fact two services of Morning Prayer and two of Evening Prayer. The services were remitted to a Revision Committee.

[2] These are in the plural as the material includes Funeral Service, Funeral of a Child, and other provision also.

[3] This 'Amending Canon' provided for completely new Canons B.1, B.2, B.3, B.4. Canon B.5 was altered but for one paragraph. A new Canon B.5A was added. The wording of Canon B.9 was altered by a few words, the first two paragraphs of Canon B.11 were altered, and a new Canon B.11A was added. Further small alterations were made in the wording of Canons B.22, B.27, B.46, B.47, B.48, C.1, C.4, C.24 and D.2. The text of the new Canons B.1 to B.5A is appended on pp.22-24 below.

[4] This 'Amending Canon' provided for a completely new Canon C.15 'Of the Declaration of Assent', and for alterations to Canons D.2, E.5, E.7, G.2 and G.4. The text of the form of 'Declaration of Assent' is appended to booklet 14A on p.24. In the House of Bishops' report to this session of Synod (GS 116B) the Bishops stated that they had deleted 'she' and inserted 'it' (referring to the Church of England), and had removed the capital from 'Him' (referring to Christ) in this Declaration of Assent. But the published text of the Canon does not include these changes!

At the **July 1975** Group of Sessions the following action was taken:
On Tuesday 1 July 1975:

Final Approval:

Series 3 Morning and Evening Prayer (for a period from 1 November 1975 to 31 December 1979):

The voting on these services was:

	Ayes	*Noes*
House of Bishops	15	0
House of Clergy	134	3
House of Laity	91	6

Series 2 (Revised) Morning and Evening Prayer (extension for a period from 28 November 1975 to 31 December 1979:

The voting on these services was:

	Ayes	*Noes*
House of Bishops	12	0
House of Clergy	75	0
House of Laity	79	1

General Consideration:

Series 1 and 2 Revised Holy Communion[1]

General Approval:

Draft Canon B.4A 'Of the Approval of Collects, Lectionaries and Table of Rules to Order the Service.'

On Friday 4 July 1975:

Promulgation and Execution of Canons:[2]

Amending Canon (No. 3) (Worship)
Amending Canon (No. 4) (Assent or Subscription to Doctrine)

Provisional Approval:

Draft Canon B.4A[3]

General Consideration:

Collects to Accompany the Lectionary for Holy Communion Series 3[4]

1 This service was then remitted to a Revision Committee. Synod was prorogued after this Group of Sessions, but the Revision Committee was kept in being.

2 Canons (not at this stage 'draft') are 'Promulged and Executed' after receiving the Queen's assent for which the Synod petitions when it has given Final Approval to a Canon. The 'Promulgation and Execution' usually comes at the next Group of Sessions, and also has to be echoed in each Diocesan Synod. The two amending Canons came into force, under their own provisions, on the day the Church of England (Worship and Doctrine) Measure 1974 came into force, i.e. 1 September 1975.

3 This is a very simple Canon, and its first two stages were taken without a Revision Committee at the same Group of Sessions (see re 'Tuesday 1 July' above). The text of the Canon is appended on p.24 below.

4 The 'Collects' were handled in the same way as Series 1 and 2 Revised Holy Communion (see note 1 above). Their final authorization was dependent upon draft Canon B.4A (see note 3 above and p.24 below) being finally approved and promulged.

At the **November 1975** Group of Sessions the following action was taken:
On Wednesday 12 November 1975:

Final Approval:

Draft Canon B.4A 'Of the Approval of Collects, Lectionaries and Table of Rules to Order the Service'.

The Voting on this Canon was:

	Ayes	*Noes*
House of Bishops	24	0
House of Clergy	166	2
House of Laity	153	3

On Thursday 13 November 1976:

General Consideration:

Series 3 Wedding Service[1]

At the **February 1976** Group of Sessions the following action was taken:
On Wednesday 25 February 1976:

Promulgation and Execution of Canon:

Canon B.4A 'Of the Approval of Collects, Lectionaries and Table of Rules to Order the Service'.

Provisional Approval:

Series 2 Holy Communion (extension)
Series 1 and 2 Revised Holy Communion

On Friday 27 February 1976:

Proposals for an 'Alternative Service Book' were approved.

At the **July 1976** Group of Sessions the following action was taken:
On Wednesday 14 July 1976:

Final Approval:

Series 2 Holy Communion (extension for a period from 28 November 1976 to 31 December 1979)

The voting on this service was:

	Ayes	*Noes*
House of Bishops	21	0
House of Clergy	134	0
House of Laity	140	0

Series 1 and 2 Revised Holy Communion (for a period from 1 November 1976 to 31 December 1979)

The voting on this service was:

	Ayes	*Noes*
House of Bishops	29	0
House of Clergy	105	52
House of Laity	115	35

Provisional Approval:

Series 3 Holy Communion (extension)
Series 3 Funeral Services (extension)
Collects to Accompany the Lectionary for Holy Communion Series 3

[1] This was then remitted to Revision Committee.

APPENDIX 3 THE NEW ICET TEXTS

As mentioned on page 6 above the 1974 ICET texts were published in July 1975 in *Prayers We Have in Common* (S.P.C.K. 65p). This booklet is called the 'Second Revised Edition', following the 'Revised Edition' of 1971. There are no apparent plans to revise texts again, so that these new texts constitute the most mature thinking of the Consultation. The changes from the 1971 texts are:

1 The Lord's Prayer: Line 2: Holy] Hallowed[1]
Line 9: Do not bring us to the test] Save us from the time of trial[2]

2 Apostles' Creed: Unchanged

3 Nicene Creed: Line 4: is seen] is, seen
Line 11: one in Being] of one Being
Line 16: was born of] became incarnate from
became] was made
Line 18: suffered, died] suffered death
Line 20: in fulfilment of] in accordance with

4 Gloria in Excelsis: Unchanged

5 Salutation and Sursum Corda: Line 4: up] OMIT

6 Sanctus and Benedictus qui Venit: Unchanged

7 Agnus Dei: Unchanged

8 Gloria Patri: Line 2: as in the beginning, so now, and for ever] as it was in the beginning, is now, and will be for ever[3]

9 Benedictus: Line 18: forgiving them] the forgiveness of
Line 22: on] into

10 Te Deum: Line 17: eternal Son] the eternal Son
Line 19: shrink from] spurn
Line 24: to the help] and help
Line 27: everlasting glory] glory everlasting
Line 10: *R.:* May we never be confounded] and we shall never hope in vain

11 Magnificat: Line 4: and] OMIT
Line 6: holy] and holy
Line 14: has sent the rich] the rich he has sent

12 Nunc Dimittis: First three lines are rewritten as:
Lord, now you let your servant go in peace;
your word has been fulfilled:
my own eyes have seen the salvation

[1] Series 3 adopted this reading in July 1972.

[2] Series 3 adopted in July 1972 the reading 'Do not bring us to the time of trial.'

[3] Series 3 Morning and Evening Prayer reads 'as it was in the beginning is now: and shall be for ever.' (Note that the corrigendum sheet to *Further Anglican Liturgies 1968-1975* missed the alteration of the last clause here).

APPENDIX 4 REVISED CANONS B.1 to B.5A

(Section B of the Canons is headed 'DIVINE SERVICE AND THE ADMINISTRALION OF THE SACRAMENTS' and those printed below are the main ones revised by the text of 'Amending Canon No. 3 (Worship and Doctrine)'. Canon B.4A in Appendix 5 was approved later,[1] and should now be inserted after B.4).

B.1 OF CONFORMITY OF WORSHIP

1. The following forms of service shall be authorised for use in the Church of England:
(a) the forms of service contained in the Book of Common Prayer;
(b) the shortened forms of Morning and Evening Prayer which were set out in the Schedule to the Act of Uniformity Amendment Act 1872;
(c) the form of service authorised by Royal Warrant for use upon the anniversary of the day of the accession of the reigning Sovereign; and
(d) any forms of service approved under Canon B.2 or Canon B.4 subject to any amendments so approved.

2. Every minister shall use only the authorised services aforesaid, except so far as he may exercise the discretion allowed to him by Canon B.5.

B.2 OF THE APPROVAL OF FORMS OF SERVICE

1. It shall be lawful for the General Synod:
(a) to approve forms of services for use in the Church of England and to amend any form of service approved by the General Synod under this Canon;
(b) to approve the use of any such form of service for a limited period, or without limit of period;
(c) to extend the period of use of any such form of service and to discontinue any such form of service;

and any form of service or amendment thereof approved by the General Synod under this Canon shall be such as in the opinion of the General Synod is neither contrary to, nor indicative of any departure from, the doctrine of the Church of England in any essential matter.

2. Any approval, amendment, continuance or discontinuance of any form of service shall not have effect unless the form of service or the amendment, continuance, or discontinuance thereof is finally approved by the General Synod with a majority in each House thereof of not less than two-thirds of those present and voting.

B.3 OF THE FORM OF SERVICE TO BE USED WHERE ALTERNATIVE FORMS ARE AUTHORISED

1. Decisions as to which of the forms of service authorised by Canon B.1, other than the services known as occasional offices, are to be used in any church in a parish or in any guild church shall be taken jointly by the minister and the parochial church council or, as the case may be, by the vicar of the guild church and the guild church council. In this Canon 'church' includes any building or part of a building licensed by the bishop for public worship according to the rites and ceremonies of the Church of England.

2. If there is disagreement as to which of the said forms of service are to be used in any such church, then, so long as the disagreement continues the forms of service to be used in that church shall be those contained in the Book of Common Prayer unless other forms of service authorised by Canon B.1 were in regular use therein during at

[1] See p.8 above.

least two of the four years immediately preceding the date when the disagreement arose and the parochial church council or guild church council, as the case may be, resolves that those other forms of service shall be used either to the exclusion of, or in addition to, the forms of service contained in the said Book.

3. The foregoing paragraphs of this Canon shall not apply in relation to a cathedral which is a parish church nor to any part of a cathedral which is a parish church.

4. Where more than one form of any of the services known as occasional offices, other than the Order of Confirmation, is authorised by Canon B.1 for use on any occasion the decision as to which form of service is to be used shall be made by the minister who is to conduct the service, but if any of the persons concerned objects beforehand to the use of the service selected by the minister and he and the minister cannot agree as to which form is to be used, the matter shall be referred to the bishop of the diocese for his decision.

B.4 OF FORMS OF SERVICE APPROVED BY THE CONVOCATIONS, ARCHBISHOPS OR ORDINARY FOR USE ON CERTAIN OCCASIONS

1. The Convocations of Canterbury and York may approve within their respective provinces forms of service for use in any cathedral or church or elsewhere on occasions for which no provision is made in the Book of Common Prayer or by the General Synod under Canon B.2, being forms of service which in both words and order are in their opinion reverent and seemly and neither contrary to, nor indicative of any departure from, the doctrine of the Church of England in any essential matter.

2. The archbishops may approve forms of service for use in any cathedral or church or elsewhere in the provinces of Canterbury and York on occasions for which no provision is made in the Book of Common Prayer or by the General Synod under Canon B.2 or by the Convocations under this Canon, being forms of service which in both words and order are in their opinion reverent and seemly and are neither contrary to, nor indicative of any departure from, the doctrine of the Church of England in any essential matter.

3. The Ordinary, subject to any regulations made from time to time by the Convocation of the province within which his jurisdiction lies, may approve forms of service for use in any cathedral or church or elsewhere in the diocese on occasions for which no provision is made in the Book of Common Prayer or by the General Synod under Canon B.2 or by the Convocation or archbishops under this Canon, being forms of service which in the opinion of the Ordinary in both words and order are reverent and seemly and are neither contrary to, nor indicative of any departure from, the doctrine of the Church of England in any essential matter.

B.5 OF THE DISCRETION OF THE MINISTER IN CONDUCT OF PUBLIC PRAYER

1. The minister may in his discretion make and use variations which are not of substantial importance in any form of service authorised by Canon B.1 according to particular circumstances.

2. Subject to any regulation made from time to time by the Convocation of the province, the minister may on occasions for which no provision is made in the Book of Common Prayer or by the General Synod under Canon B.2 or by the Convocation, archbishops, or Ordinary under Canon B.4 use forms of service considered suitable by him for those occasions.

3. All variations in forms of service and all forms of service used under this Canon shall be reverent and seemly and shall be neither contrary to, nor indicative of any departure from, the doctrine of the Church of England in any essential matter.

4. If any question is raised concerning the observance of the provisions of the last preceding paragraph or whether a variation in a form of service is of substantial importance or not, it may be referred to the bishop in order that he may give such pastoral guidance or advice as he may think fit, but such reference shall be without prejudice to the matter in question being made the subject-matter of proceedings under the Ecclesiastical Jurisdiction Measure 1963.

B.5A OF AUTHORISATION FOR THE USE OF A SERVICE IN DRAFT FORM
Where a form of service is in course of preparation with a view to its submission to the General Synod for approval by the Synod under Canon B.2, the archbishops may authorise that service in draft form to be conducted by a minister in the presence of a congregation consisting of such persons only as the archbishops may designate.

APPENDIX 5 NEW CANON B.4A

B.4A OF THE APPROVAL OF COLLECTS, LECTIONARIES AND TABLE OF RULES TO ORDER THE SERVICE.

1. It shall be lawful for the General Synod:
(a) to approve new forms of the prayers known as collects, or any of them, for use in any service approved under Canon B.2 or Canon B.4 and to amend any form of collect approved by the General Synod under this Canon;
(b) to approve the use of any such form of collect for a limited period or without limit of period;
(c) to extend the period of use of any form of collect so approved and to discontinue any such form;
and any form of collect or amendment thereof approved by the General Synod under this Canon shall be such as in the opinion of the General Synod is neither contrary to, nor indicative of any departure from, the doctrine of the Church of England in any essential matter.

2. It shall be lawful for the General Synod:
(a) to approve Tables of Lessons for use in any service approved by the General Synod under Canon B.2 and to amend any such Table approved by the General Synod under this sub-paragraph;
(b) to approve a Table of Rules for regulating the Service when two Holy Days fall upon the same day or their Proper Services otherwise fall together, or when necessary for any other reason, and to amend any such Table approved by the General Synod under this sub-paragraph.
(c) to approve the use of any such Table as is mentioned in sub-paragraph (a) or (b) of this paragraph for a limited period or without limit of period.
(d) to extend the period of use of any such Table so approved and to discontinue any such Table.
In this paragraph 'Holy Day' means the Day set out in 'A Table of all the Feasts' in the Book of Common Prayer and such other Days as the General Synod considers should be included in any Table of Rules approved under this paragraph.

3. Any approval, amendment, continuance or discontinuance of any form of collect, or of any such Table as is mentioned in sub-paragraph (a) or (b) of paragraph 2 of this Canon, shall not have effect unless the form of collect or the Table, or the amendment, continuance or discontinuance thereof, is finally approved by the General Synod with a majority in each House thereof of not less than two-thirds of those present and voting.

GROVE BOOKLETS ON MINISTRY AND WORSHIP

Published one each month—24 (or more) pages. Titles asterisked are in second edition or a reprint. Cost **25p** (or **30p**—and all are **30p** from 1 September, 1976). Nos. 4, 11 and 17 are not available. Send for catalogue.

- *1. **The Anglican-Roman Catholic Agreement on the Eucharist** by Julian W. Charley
- *2. **Ministry in the Local Church** by P. A. Crowe, A. R. Henderson and J. I. Packer
- *3. **Baptismal Discipline (Revised Edition)** by Colin Buchanan
- *5. **A Service of Thanksgiving and Blessing** by C. H. B. Byworth and J. A. Simpson. (Also Service Sheet only **5p** or **45p** per dozen and Certificate **4p**)
- 6. **Informal Liturgy** by Trevor Lloyd
- *7. **The Church and the Gifts of the Spirit** by John Goldingay
- *8. **Communion, Confirmation and Commitment (Revised Edition)** by C. H. B. Byworth
- *9. **Patterns of Sunday Worship** by Colin Buchanan
- *10. **A Guide to Series 3** by Peter E. Dale
- *12. **The Language of Series 3** by David L. Frost
- 13. **What Priesthood has the Ministry?** by J. M. R. Tillard
- 14. **Recent Liturgical Revision in the Church of England** by Colin Buchanan
- 14A. **Supplement for 1973-4 to Recent Liturgical Revision in the Church of England** by Colin Buchanan
- 14B. **Supplement for 1974-6 to Recent Liturgical Revision in the Church of England** by Colin Buchanan (**30p**)
- 15. **Institutions and Inductions** by Trevor Lloyd
- 16. **Alternative Eucharistic Prayers** by Derek Billings
- 18. **Community, Prayer and the Individual** by Peter R. Akehurst
- 19. **Agapes and Informal Eucharists** by Trevor Lloyd
- 20. **A case for Infant Baptism** by Colin Buchanan
- 21. **Evangelistic Services** by Michael H. Botting
- 22. **Agreement on the Doctrine of the Ministry** by Julian W. Charley
- 23. **A Modern Liturgical Bibliography** by John E. Tiller
- *24. **Infant Baptism under Cross-Examination** by David Pawson and Colin Buchanan (**30p**)
- 25. **Send us out** by Peter E. Dale
- 26. **Music for the Parish** by Sidney Green and Gordon Ogilvie
- 27. **Ministry and Death** by Trevor Lloyd
- 28. **Liturgy and Death** by Trevor Lloyd
- 29. **The Ordinal and its Revision** by Peter Toon
- 30. **Liturgy and Creation** by Peter R. Akehurst
- 31. **Christian Education on Sunday Mornings.** Edited by Charles Hutchins
- 32. **Inaugural Services.** Edited by Colin Buchanan
- 33. **Knowing God through the Liturgy** by Peter Toon
- 34. **Modern Roman Catholic Worship: The Mass** by Nicholas Sagovsky
- 35. **Drama in Worship** by Andy Kelso
- 36. **Praying Aloud Together** by Peter R. Akehurst
- 37. **The Liturgy for Infant Baptism (Series 3)** by Colin Buchanan
- *38. **Open to God** by Tom Walker
- 39. **Worship and Silence** by Margaret Harvey
- 40. **Freedom in a Framework: Some Possibilities with Series 3** by Richard More
- 41. **Keeping Holy Week** by Peter R. Akehurst (**30p**)
- 42. **Christian Healing in the Parish** by Michael Botting (**30p**)
- 43. **Modern Roman Catholic Worship: Baptism and Penance** by Nicholas Sagovsky (**30p**)
- 44. **Exorcism, Deliverance and Healing: Some Pastoral Guidelines** by John Richards (**30p**)
- 45. **Equipping God's People: Present and Future Parish Training Schemes** by Peter Lee (August 1976) (**30p**)
- 46. **Authority and the Ministry** by John Goldingay (October 1976) (**30p**)
- 47. **Liturgy for Marriage: Some Guidelines with Reference to the Series 3 Service** by Charles H. Hutchins (November 1976) (**30p**)

ISSN 0305 3067 ISBN 0 901710 94 6

GROVE BOOKS

BRAMCOTE NOTTS. (0602-251114)

Printed by Hassall & Lucking Ltd., Cross Street, Long Eaton, Nottingham NG10 1HD Tel. L.E. 3292

The GODHEAD

(REVISED)

By Kenneth V. Reeves